FROM FACTORY TO TABLE
WHAT YOU'RE REALLY EATING™

THE TRUTH BEHIND
FACTORY
FOODS

JULIA J. QUINLAN AND PAULA JOHANSON

rosen publishing's
rosen
central®

New York

For the people at the Green Future discussion, who are making good choices
—Paula Johanson

Published in 2018 by The Rosen Publishing Group, Inc.
29 East 21st Street, New York, NY 10010

Library of Congress Cataloging-in-Publication Data

Names: Quinlan, Julia J., author. | Johanson, Paula, author.
Title: The truth behind factory foods / Julia J. Quinlan and Paula Johanson.
Description: New York : Rosen Central, 2018. | Series: From factory to table:
what you're really eating | Audience: Grades 5–8. | Includes bibliographical
references and index.
Identifiers: LCCN 2017020111 | ISBN 9781499439250 (library bound) | ISBN
9781499439236 (pbk.) | ISBN 9781499439243 (6 pack)
Subjects: LCSH: Convenience foods—Juvenile literature.
Classification: LCC TX370 .Q56 2018 | DDC 641/.2—dc23
LC record available at https://lccn.loc.gov/2017020111

Manufactured in China

CONTENTS

Much of the food we eat today is made in factories. These foods are then put on trucks, ships, and airplanes and sent around the country and world. We are a long way from our ancestors who grew food on their own land and ate what they grew. Factory-produced foods are commonly known as processed foods. Of course, you can still find whole, unprocessed food. Fruits, vegetables, and eggs are not processed.

Processed, or factory, foods are popular because they are cheap and quick to get on your plate. They are also convenient. Who wants to spend the time making meatballs when you can buy a bag of twenty frozen meatballs in the frozen food section? Some of the most popular factory food is what people buy at fast-food restaurants.

While these foods are fast and cheap, they are not the best for our health. When foods are processed, they often have additives, sweeteners, and preservatives added in. Many of these foods are marketed to adults trying to lose weight and young people. Foods marketed as "low fat" are indeed low in fat, but they are often full of high fructose corn syrup and other sweeteners. These sweeteners make low-fat foods taste better, but sugar is converted into fat once it is in the body. Many processed foods, such as candy, fruit snacks, and cereal, have fun cartoon characters associated with them. They are packaged in brightly colored bags and boxes, which are appealing to young people. However, these foods are full of sugar and not healthy to eat regularly.

Eating too much factory food can have serious long-term health effects and even negative short-

There are plenty of whole foods in the produce section of the supermarket. Fruits and vegetables are healthy choices and can be made into delicious meals without too much work.

term effects. Luckily, it is easy to make healthier choices without missing out on your favorite foods. Eating primarily whole foods and reading nutrition labels is a good start. All packaged food has a nutrition label on the back. It's a good idea to take a look at the label before buying a product. Read the ingredients and see if you understand what they are. Look and see how much sugar, fat, and sodium is in the item. If you are craving french fries and a hamburger from your favorite fast-food restaurant, try making them at home. There are potatoes in the produce section and hamburger

Fast food can be nice to have as a treat once in a while. But these heavily processed foods should not be eaten regularly.

meat in the meat section. Many people often resort to factory foods when they are looking for a quick snack. Part of healthy eating is planning ahead. Bring bags of nuts or baby carrots with you so you have something quick on hand for when you get hungry.

Processed, unhealthy foods are all around us. Learning how they're made, their health consequences, and healthy alternatives is a great first step in making a positive change in how you eat.

CHAPTER ONE

THE PROCESS OF PROCESSING

Y ou won't find processed foods growing on trees or in fields. They are made by people. Some of the most popular fast foods are hamburgers, french fries, tacos, soda, cereal, fried chicken, and pizza. All of these fast foods are also processed. The ways that processed foods, fried foods, and fast foods are made can be astonishing. There are a lot of questions worth asking before you eat something. What's in this food? Where did it come from? Who made it?

WHAT'S IN THAT BURGER?

Hamburgers can be real, healthy food, made from meat that is raised without the use of antibiotics and hormones. A good hamburger is served on a whole grain bun with toppings such as romaine lettuce or spinach and slices of tomato and onion. It takes several minutes to cook a hamburger and serve it on a plate with freshly sliced toppings.

Most fast-food hamburgers are made from high-fat meat that is ground up with bits of tough meat and gristle. Most American fast-food hamburger patties are made in one of

Hamburgers made at home with fresh ingredients are a healthy and delicious alternative to fast food.

only fifteen large slaughterhouses. The meat inspectors are kept so busy that they have time to check only one side of a carcass for tumors and injuries. The biggest hamburger restaurant chains in the United States don't buy young cattle for meat. They save money by using old dairy cows that have been used for breeding and milking. Often, dairy cows are given growth hormones to increase milk production. The bits of meat from hundreds of carcasses are ground together, shaped into patties, and frozen in a factory.

Most of these patties are fried in grease on a griddle and kept warm until a kitchen worker places the patties on buns made from bleached white flour. A squirt of sweet ketchup and a sprinkle of mechanically diced onion are no substitutes for fresh toppings. A few shreds of iceberg lettuce have almost no nutritional value. The fast-food version of a hamburger may be easy to buy, but it's quite different from real food.

FATTY FRENCH FRIES

French fries from fast-food restaurants aren't cut from fresh potatoes like the homemade version. Commercially made french fries are lightly boiled, frozen, and then packaged to be trucked hundreds of miles to various restaurants. In some factories, french fries are shaped out of cooked mashed potatoes. Restaurants cook the frozen fries in vats of hot fat—animal or vegetable oil. Most restaurants change the oil every week or two. The used fat is sometimes recycled to make lipstick.

Fast-food restaurants use baskets, like this one, to submerge frozen french fries in vats of fat.

A popular international restaurant chain used to use a combination of beef tallow and pork lard to cook french fries. When customers found out, many communities were outraged and disgusted. People assumed the fries were cooked in vegetable oil. Both Muslim and Jewish traditions forbid the eating of pork. These religions prepare their food in special ways called halal and kosher, respectively. Pigs are considered unclean in both religions. Moreover, people who keep kosher do not mix meat and milk in the same meal. In Hindu traditions, beef products are not eaten because cows are regarded as holy animals. Vegetarian customers insisted that vegetable oil should be used instead of animal products. The restaurant chain found that its french fries tasted different when they did not use beef fat, so in many countries the chain adds hydrolyzed beef flavor to the potatoes. This restaurant chain is now trying to please some of its customers in some countries. But food laws don't make restaurants print this specific information on their menus.

FOOD SAFETY

Governments try to control how food is prepared by passing laws and regulations. These rules are supposed to ensure that food is prepared and handled safely. If food is not kept at the correct temperature, germs can begin to grow. These germs can cause food-borne illnesses. These germs can grow in hot food that's kept barely warm before being served or cold food that's kept at room temperature instead of in a cold refrigerator.

Tacos are a good example of fast food that needs to be kept at the proper temperature. Fried ground meat must be kept hot, until the taco is put together. The trimmings of chopped lettuce and tomatoes and grated cheese must be kept cold. The spicy sauce could be kept cold or hot, not room temperature. Workers

EASY ISN'T BETTER

Running into your local corner store or convenience store for a snack is really easy. They have chips, cookies, candy, and soda. You can be in and out in five minutes. However, that quick snack can have lasting health effects. These processed snacks are full of sugar and salt. They also lack nutritional value. A handful of nuts or fruit offers many nutritional benefits. They have fiber, protein, and vitamins. Whole food snacks will also keep you full longer and give you more energy. So, keep in mind that what's easy in the short term may not be what's best in the long term.

must have clean hands or clean gloves, and the kitchen must be kept clean. It can be a challenge to keep each food item at the correct temperature until it is served.

Over two-thirds of restaurants "had at least one high-risk food safety violation," according to a survey conducted by the Center for Science in the Public Interest (CSPI) in twenty US cities. "The most critical violations cited included: 26 percent of restaurants were cited for contaminated food contact surfaces, 22 percent of restaurants were cited for improper holding temperatures, 16 percent of restaurants were cited for inadequate hand washing by employees, 13 percent of restaurants were cited for rodent/insect activity." It's not enough to have laws about clean hands, clean kitchens, and the appropriate temperature to store and serve food. Restaurants must be inspected regularly and made to do the right thing.

ANSWER THIS!

Question: How much sugar is in a soft drink? Answer: More than you might think, probably more than you can believe. Most people who make a sweet drink such as iced tea at home add one or two spoonfuls of sugar. But cans of iced tea contain 7 or more teaspoons (34.5 milliliters) of sugar. The average can of soda pop has up to 12 teaspoons (59.2 ml) of sugar. Drinking just one can of soda each day adds a lot of empty calories to a person's diet. These calories are called empty because they do not include any nutritional value. When you drink milk, you are ingesting calories but also vitamins, minerals, and protein. Soda is not something that should be drunk regularly. What's worse is that more than a third of all soda sold in North America is had as a drink with breakfast and lunch, instead of milk or water.

CEREAL: NOT SO SIMPLE

A bowl of cereal is a simple, fast breakfast. But it's a good idea to read the ingredients listed on the box before deciding whether it is a real breakfast food.

Many packaged cereals have two or three times as much sugar and salt as people would add to oatmeal, porridge, or granola they make at home. Artificial food coloring and flavoring are added to some cereals to make them interesting to children. Packaged cereal is often made from bleached white flour, not whole wheat flour. Corn flour, sweeteners made from corn, and salt are usually added. There are also chemical preservatives added to most packaged cereals, which aren't needed for bags of dry oatmeal, cornmeal, or cracked grain porridge.

Some packaged cereals are made from healthier whole wheat. But look carefully at the rest of the ingredients! At least seven popular whole-grain cereals are promoted as being "fortified" with minerals. These minerals come from the additive trisodium phosphate (TSP). The chemical TSP is an industrial cleaner that is used to remove oil stains. It is also used in toilet bowl cleaner, laundry soap, and dishwasher detergent.

FOOD TO GO, SICKNESS TO STAY

Many people don't have the time or desire to make their own pizza or chicken nuggets. For these people, fast-food restaurants are where they go to get these foods. These take-out foods may look like food someone would cook at home, but look carefully! Take-out restaurants use twice as much salt, or more, as anyone does at home. Corn syrup is added to pizza sauce and to batter for fried chicken. Only a few restaurants have recipes with little or no salt and sweetener added.

Besides the health issues associated with eating fast food, many people are ethically opposed to how the animals used in fast food are treated. The chickens used to make chicken nuggets and the cattle used to make hamburgers are kept in terrible conditions. On factory farms, pigs are kept in crowded pens. Their tails are removed so they don't bite each other out of boredom. Some pigs are kept in small cages all their lives. On factory farms, chickens are crowded into barns and kept in cages that are stacked one on top of the other. Chickens raised

Chickens raised for factory foods are usually kept inside their whole lives. Some people prefer to eat meat from chickens that were raised free range, or allowed to move around both inside and outside.

for meat are fed hormones that make them grow so quickly that their legs are not strong enough to hold up their big, meaty chests. Factory farm animals' food grain is mixed with leftover animal parts from slaughterhouses.

These animals are fed hormones and antibiotics and suffer for most of their lives. This is where the phrase "you are what you eat" becomes important. When we eat meat, eggs, or milk from animals raised in these conditions, we are ingesting everything they have eaten. Nutritionist Marion Nestle collected research that showed that eating the animals and products of animals raised on factory farms can cause health problems and allergies in humans. "How are we treating the animals we eat while they're alive," asks Michael Pollan, "and then how humanely are we 'dispatching' them?"

CHAPTER TWO

FACTORY FOOD IN YOUR BODY

Have you ever heard of empty calories? It means that the calories being ingested have no nutritional value. The body needs a variety of nutrients, which come from food or drinks containing calories, on a daily basis in order to function. Nutrients make our bodies healthy. We can get calcium from milk, which makes our bones strong, and fiber from beans, which helps our digestion. Children and young adults need even more nutrients because they are still growing. Fake foods have fewer or even no nutrients. Eating too many fake foods can have a negative effect on our bodies. Without nutrients, people have difficulty building strong muscles and growing. A lack of nutrients can also make it difficult to recover from a cold or another illness. Even day to day, the bad effects of eating fake foods can be noticed. For example, many people who eat a lot of sugary and starchy food find they develop more pimples. Going to the bathroom can become complicated—too much salt and sugar make people dehydrated and constipated.

The effect of even one meal can be considerable. People training for athletic events often load up on complex carbohydrates the day before the event to ensure that they have a lot of energy available. But fake foods can be full of sugar and are no substitute for whole-grain pasta with healthy homemade sauce.

NOT SO SWEET

There are some kinds of sugar that are naturally in fruits and vegetables. Many factory foods have added processed sugars instead of natural juice sweeteners. Factory foods lack fiber, which helps the body slowly digest sugar. Sweet fake food without fiber, such as candy or soda, allow sugar to be digested quickly. If sugar gets into the bloodstream quickly, as is the case with processed foods, the pancreas has to speed up and make enzymes quickly to process all that sugar. This makes blood sugar rise quickly and creates a burst of energy. However, this burst does not last because blood sugar drops just as quickly. When this happens, we feel weak and tired. This is commonly known as a sugar rush.

Processed sweets have a lot of high-fructose corn syrup added.

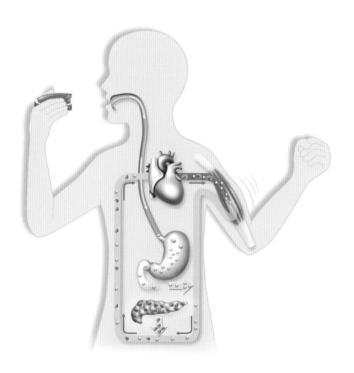

Here you can see sugar traveling down to the pancreas. Eating too much sugar puts a lot of stress on the pancreas.

These foods cause something called rebound hunger; an hour or so after eating, the body is hungry again. This rebound hunger increases the risk of becoming overweight or obese because it causes people to eat more frequently. Rebound hunger affects a person's mind, too. Studies of students have found that alertness and learning potential drops after the first hour for those who have soft drinks and sugary cereal for breakfast.

EASY FOOD, DIFFICULT DIGESTION

That uncomfortable feeling after eating greasy fried food isn't just from being too full. It's from the gallbladder trying to make extra digestive fluids. Stressed gallbladders form lumps called gallstones, which can restrict or block the duct connecting the liver, gallbladder, and pancreas to the upper part of the intestine. Most American adults eat so much fat that many of them have small gallstones and don't know it. This is also common in many overweight children.

FAKE FAT?

Because eating too much fat is bad for people's health, doctors have been researching solutions. One invention is fake fat or fat substitutes. Scientists have been able to alter the long chains of molecules that make up fat so that it is not digestible. The idea is that the fat will not be digested and won't make people gain weight. While this sounds like a good idea, this fake fat can have negative effects on the body.

The fake fat turns into lumps that don't move easily through the colon. This makes it hard to have a bowel movement. People can get cramps and become constipated. Additionally, as

EVERYTHING IN MODERATION

Every body is different and it is important to know what works best for you. There are some people who cannot eat any processed foods without feeling sick. Some people think it is morally wrong to eat food they don't grow themselves, and some people eat nothing but processed foods! While it is not healthy to eat processed foods exclusively, it is not dangerous, for most people, to have some once in a while. What is most important is to have a balanced diet that consists primarily of vegetables and whole grains.

solid waste gets packed into the lower colon, the fake fat can make liquid waste that leaks around the solid waste. This can lead to unintended waste leakage. Some foods have warnings of "anal leakage."

WATCH OUT WHEN EATING OUT

People who work in restaurants are food professionals, and customers depend on them. "On a typical day, 44 percent of American adults eat at a restaurant. Unfortunately, the rate of food-borne illness from restaurant food is disturbingly high," wrote Sarah Klein and Caroline Smith DeWaal in "Dirty Dining," a report for the CSPI. "Data from 1990 through 2006 indicate that 41 percent of all food-borne illness outbreaks can be traced to restaurant food, compared to 22 percent from private homes."

E. coli-related food poisoning is one of the most common food-borne illnesses. In healthy people, it causes a couple days of discomfort, with nausea, vomiting, and diarrhea. The more severe form known as E. coli 0157:H7 causes bloody diarrhea and may cause life-threatening kidney failure. Other food-borne illnesses are caused by germs, such as norovirus, salmonella, clostridium, and botulism. Norovirus infections are also known as Norwalk viruses (after Norwalk, Ohio, where an outbreak of the virus was first identified in 1972). Nurses commonly joke that patients who

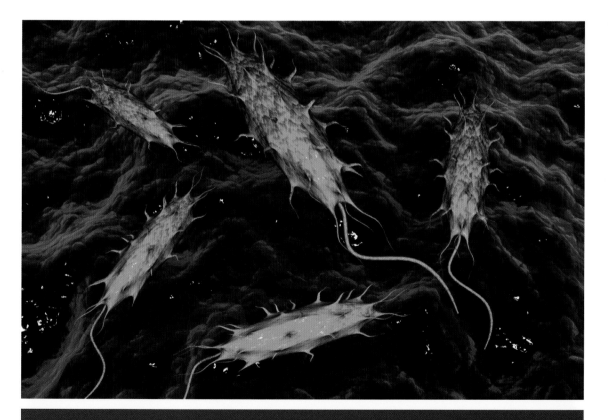

This is a microscopic image of E. coli. These tiny bacteria can cause huge problems for people who ingest them.

have food poisoning are "Norwalking" when they sit on a toilet, with diarrhea while holding a bucket for vomiting.

How does restaurant food make people sick? In "Dirty Dining," Klein and DeWaal quote a report from the U.S. Food and Drug Administration (FDA) that says 75 percent of restaurant employees do not wash their hands or don't do so satisfactorily. They also note that "There can be as many germs beneath a ring, for example, as there are people in Europe."

Some kinds of food-borne illness such as listeriosis, caused by *Listeria* bacteria, are spread on contaminated machines and surfaces in factories, where food is cut and packaged. *Listeria* is usually found in soil and water. Animals eat food or drink water that is contaminated with *Listeria*. People who eat the meat from these animals get very ill if the meat hasn't been cooked at a high enough temperature to kill the bacteria. Milk is pasteurized to kill bacteria. But people's hands are a more common way for food-borne illnesses to spread. "Three pathogens come primarily from infected workers: Hepatitis A virus, and *Shigella* and *Staphylococcus aureus* bacteria," Klein and DeWaal point out. "Hepatitis A and *Shigella* are carried in human fecal matter [bodily waste]. The illnesses they cause can be prevented by proper hand washing."

PACKAGING THE PLANET

Fast food is usually wrapped in disposable wrappers. These wrappers are easy to throw away, but unlike regular paper, they take a long time to disintegrate, or break down. The soft plastic of the wrappers is full of chemicals, such as phthalates, that can make food taste like plastic. The chemicals from the wrappers can leach into food. These chemicals have effects similar to hormones on people's bodies. Scientists are still trying to learn how

Landfills, like this one, are full of plastics that are not biodegradable. They pose a big risk to the environment. It is important to recycle and reduce the use of nonrecyclable packaging.

quickly these chemicals can have an effect on the human body. Since they act like hormones, they can alter people's moods and overall health. These hormonelike chemicals can also have a serious effect on children, like changing the timing of puberty. Some girls are now experiencing puberty earlier than in previous generations. It is also becoming more common for young boys to have swollen breasts.

MYTHS AND FACTS

MYTH

It's too expensive to eat healthy and buy fresh foods.

FACT

Fresh, healthy foods are cheaper in a couple of ways. Eating healthy saves money on medical bills; heart attacks, diabetes, strokes, cancer, and depression caused by a diet high in processed food cost a lot to treat. Also, fresh food is cheaper per bite.

MYTH

Fried chicken from a fast-food restaurant is just like the chicken we make at home.

FACT

When you cook at home, you can choose what ingredients to use. Homemade fried chicken can be made from organic, free-range chicken and you can limit the amount of salt and fat used. Fried chicken made at a fast-food restaurant is made however that restaurant makes it. Most likely, deep fried in fat and full of additives. It's much easier to be healthy when you know what you're eating.

MYTH

Advertisements don't work and don't change peoples' buying habits.

FACT

Marketers and advertisers know how to influence peoples' decisions. Most people are influenced by ads, even if they don't realize it.

CHAPTER THREE

AN APPLE A DAY...

We've all heard the saying "an apple a day keeps the doctor away," it means that eating healthily will keep our bodies healthy and we won't have to go to the doctor as much. An unhealthy diet can make us sick.

Health is not just important to individual people but to society as a whole. In his book *Food Rules: An Eater's Manual*, Michael Pollan writes that "Populations that eat a so-called Western diet—generally defined as a diet consisting of lots of processed foods...invariably suffer from high rates of the so-called Western diseases: obesity, type 2 diabetes, cardiovascular disease and cancer." By looking at the lives of thousands of people,

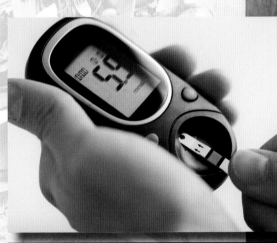

People with diabetes use meters, such as this one, to measure their blood sugar level.

doctors are learning how to diagnose what makes whole societies healthy or ill.

Eating mostly fast food and processed food can cause more than just a day or two of diarrhea or constipation. Long-term constipation and diarrhea lead to the formation of hemorrhoids and contribute to diverticulosis, diverticulitis, and colon cancer. These are chronic conditions that cause a lot of pain and can be deadly. These conditions also make people feel uncomfortable and embarrassed.

FOOD FOR NOW, HEALTH FOREVER

Food poisoning from salmonella or other germs can cause long-term complications, such as reactive arthritis, also known as Reiter's syndrome. This illness causes inflamed joints, eyes, and urethras. Many doctors remember this illness by the rhyme "The patient can't see, can't pee, can't bend the knee." The deep, aching pain is often severe and requires hospitalization. Some patients need several shots of morphine each day for weeks while in the hospital. Some are still too sore a year later to turn a key in a car's ignition or too stiff to put on a coat without assistance. Bill Marler, a lawyer who works to help people who have been harmed by food-borne illnesses, writes, "General sanitary techniques of hand washing and clean drinking water have decreased the incidence of these infections in industrialized countries, but they are still very prevalent in less developed countries and the third world." Symptoms of severe arthritis can be permanent.

Digesting a single fatty fried meal can cause lasting problems. A gallstone that previously caused no side effects may suddenly block the duct and cause permanent damage to both the gallbladder and pancreas. Blocked ducts can lead

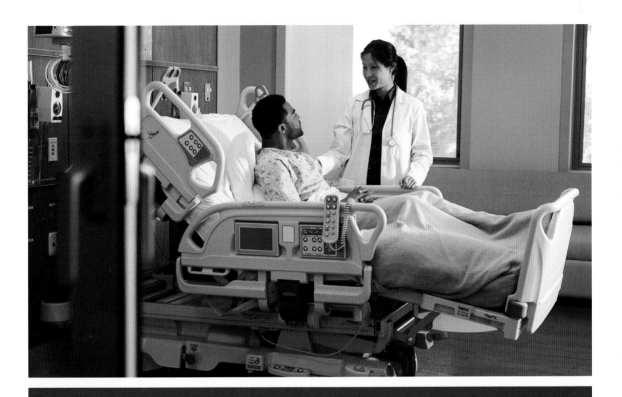

You might not think that a quick meal at your favorite restaurant could land you in the hospital, but it's possible. It could be from salmonella poisoning or diabetes.

to appendicitis, pancreas failure, and diabetes. The pain of an inflamed pancreas is caused by enzymes leaking out, which digest some of the body's own tissues. People who ignore that pain aren't tough and brave; they're risking surgery, chronic pain, and diabetes. People can end up needing to take pills or give themselves a shot every day for the rest of their lives because the pancreas no longer makes enough enzymes or insulin.

Fake foods can be especially risky for people who have allergies. Even the best fast-food restaurants often mix up food orders and ingredients. For someone with an allergy, it's

Restaurants are busy places full of customers and workers. In these hectic conditions, food safety can be overlooked and sickness can spread.

hard to know for sure if any restaurant has prepared food that is safe to eat. In addition, most processed food contains the common allergens corn, soybeans, wheat, and milk products. Factories often process many different foods. Factories that process nuts and peanuts can accidentally put crumbs into other products when they use the same machinery. People who have food allergies have to read labels very carefully. Some people have hives and stomachaches for weeks after inadvertently eating a food containing ingredients they are allergic to. People who are severely allergic to nuts or seafood can become seriously ill or die from just the smallest amount of that allergen.

CHOICES AND HEALTH

There are many things in life we cannot control that affect our health. If you trip and sprain your ankle, it's an accident. But if you are eating deep-fried food every day, that's a choice. Choosing to eat healthy foods is something we have control over that can have a huge benefit to our health. Eating healthy reduces the risk of heart disease, diabetes, and obesity. Sometimes, it's hard to make these healthy choices because it can take a long time to see results. But it is important to make these choices because controlling diabetes, reducing blood pressure, and losing weight take even longer and are far more difficult.

DIET AND CANCER

Usually, there's no single reason why someone gets cancer. Diet is only one factor among many. However, diet is something people can change.

The Western diet includes a lot of processed, fried, and fast food. "Virtually all of the obesity and type 2 diabetes, 80 percent of the cardiovascular disease, and more than a third of all cancers can be linked to this diet," writes Michael Pollan. "In countries where people eat a pound or more of vegetables and fruits a day, the rate of cancer is half what it is in the United States."

Doctors aren't sure of precisely what in the Western diet is causing cancer and other illnesses. But it's pretty clear that there are fewer cases of cancer in people who eat more fruits and vegetables every day rather than fake foods.

FEED YOUR BRAIN

"If you've ever wondered why fatty food tastes so good, there are reasons why. Your brain and body need fat to function well," says psychologist Bruce Mansbridge. "The tissues of your brain and nerves are about 60 percent fat by weight." Eating fake foods labeled "fat free" does no good for a hungry brain.

Processed food is linked by writer Gracelyn Guyol, who was diagnosed with mild bipolar disorder, to rising rates of depression, anxiety disorders, and even epilepsy. Part of the problem with processed foods are the chemical preservatives and bad fats found in them. A packaged snack cake won't rot for a year on a store shelf but in a human body the trans fat in the cake will clog blood vessels. Certain kinds of fats are very good for brain and nerve function, but these good fats are absent from most processed and fast foods. "The fat and oils in fish are particularly good for growing and maintaining a healthy brain," according to Mansbridge. "Studies have proved the benefits of including fish oils in the diet of people being treated for depression."

FULL BUT NOT NOURISHED

People's bodies need more from food than just the feeling of a full stomach. They need many kinds of nutrients from a variety of foods. Many North Americans are now being diagnosed with chronic diseases caused by malnutrition, such as kwash-iorkor, pellagra, and beriberi. This lack of nutrients can also cause diseases like scurvy, which can cause your teeth to fall out! This can happen to people who are overweight or obese because, even though they are getting plenty of calories, they are not getting enough nutrients.

"Food companies will make and market any product that sells, regardless of its nutritional value or its effect on health," writes Marion Nestle. "In this regard, food companies hardly differ from cigarette companies."

CHAPTER FOUR

WHOLE FOODS

There are ways to make real food as appealing as fake food. Start with good flavors and interesting textures. Try new recipes and new local restaurants. Feeling healthy and nourished feels better than feeling bloated or tired. Those are good reasons to make a salad for lunch!

That's not to say that someone who eats no fruits or vegetables should start by eating a pound and a half the first day of a new diet. That could be really uncomfortable. But eating one apple the first day is a good start. Every week or so, try replacing one serving of fast food or candy each day with a handful of vegetables or a piece of fruit. In a month or two, that adds up to a lot of fresh food eaten every day.

BREAKFAST ALTERNATIVES

There are more choices for breakfast than a box of sweetened cereal, processed into brightly colored shapes. "Don't eat cereal that changes the color of the milk," advises Michael Pollan. A healthier option is to make homemade cereal using rolled oats and wheat germ. It only takes a minute to make, using a microwave or a kettle of boiling water. Fresh, dried, or frozen fruit is a great addition to plain yogurt. A breakfast wrap can be made with a whole-wheat tortilla wrapped around scrambled eggs, mushrooms, and diced peppers.

LUNCH TO GO

Lunch is a good time to start replacing fake foods with real food. Lunch food doesn't have to be bought sealed in wrappers. It's not hard to make sandwiches with whole-grain bread. Cheese, boiled eggs, and raw vegetables are easy to slice up. A casserole can be cut into individual portions and sealed in bowls

Baby carrots are a super easy, on-the-go snack. Bring some with you in a bag or container and you're ready to snack.

with lids. That's also a good way to carry salads, with a separate container for dressing. A thermos is a good way to carry homemade soup and keep it hot. There are bakeries that make muffins and cookies as good as homemade ones, with half the sugar, butter, and salt of most commercial baked goods.

Healthy snacking requires a bit more forethought, but it can be fun to prepare food with family or friends. Get snacks ready for the week ahead and you won't have to worry about having healthy snacks all week.

FAST, HEALTHY SNACKS

There are plenty of alternatives to a candy bar. Many so-called chocolate bars are actually made mostly of sugar or sweeteners manufactured from corn and are less than 12 percent chocolate. These bars don't melt on a warm day because carnauba wax is added. People who want to eat something sweet might want an orange, not a piece of shoe polish mixed with corn syrup. But many stores don't sell fresh fruit, only processed sweets sealed in plastic wrappers.

It's easy to carry an apple or an orange for a snack. Other kinds of fruit such as peaches, bananas, or grapes may need to

ADVERTISING AND MARKETING

Companies that make fast food and processed food spend a lot of money on advertising. It's important to think critically about what we see in advertisements. Often, these ads do not focus on the food itself, instead they focus on how cool or fun you'll seem if you drink a certain soda or eat a certain type of chips. But remember to think about how these fake foods will make you feel physically and their long-term effects. Ask yourself: What is being sold in this ad—real food or an attitude? It's very unusual to see an advertisement for lettuce, strawberries, or carrots. These natural foods do not need to be part of an ad campaign to trick people into buying them.

be carried in a little container. Vegetables like beans and broccoli make tasty snacks, too. There are tidy little bags of peeled carrots sold in grocery stores. It's fun to taste different fruits and vegetables as they become ripe each season.

There are salty alternatives to potato chips. One choice is natural popcorn: it's real food when people buy a bag of kernels to pop. Microwave popcorn that is advertised as having "buttery" flavor is not made with real butter but a greasy additive. It's made of artificial ingredients, including diacetyl, that can cause factory workers to get rashes, lung diseases, and even die. The National Institute for Occupational Safety and Health (NIOSH) links exposure to diacetyl to lung disease in popcorn-factory workers. The added salt is two or three times as much as most people add to a serving of popcorn.

A bag of plain kernels is much less expensive than micro-wave bags of popcorn. Popcorn kernels can be microwaved in a paper bag or popped in a hot air popper. Popcorn tastes good plain or you can drizzle a spoonful of melted butter or olive oil on top. Adding a sprinkle of garlic powder, spices, or even a table-spoon of Parmesan cheese will make it taste great! Or maybe for a birthday party, use a little melted butter and a bit of maple syrup to make sweet popcorn balls to share.

DELICIOUS AND HEALTHY DINNERS

A fast dinner doesn't have to be take-out chicken or fast-food hamburgers, not when salads and roasts are easy to make. A good way to start is by replacing one fake food dinner each week with real food. Making ordinary dinners out of real foods gets easier with practice. There are cookbooks in libraries. Ask friends and relatives how to make special cultural dishes—some people enjoy sharing recipes and cooking techniques.

Cooking meals at home might seem intim-idating, but there are many easy-to-follow recipes available in cookbooks and online.

A fun way to enjoy a number of different dishes is to hold a potluck dinner. When each person brings a different dish, no one person has to prepare the entire meal. Pizza parties are another fun idea for cooking with friends or family. Instead of having pizza delivered, start with homemade dough or a pack of whole-wheat torti-llas. Add tomato sauce and some grated cheese. Let everyone top the pizzas with peppers, tomatoes, mushrooms, or their own favorites. Look for meat from animals raised on local farms.

MEET A FARMER

A good alternative to purchasing fake food shipped from factories is to buy fresh food grown on local farms. The Slow Food movement and the 100-Mile Diet both encourage people to enjoy seasonal foods that are locally grown. Farmers markets bring fresh produce to customers in cities and towns. "For 300 years, this country's family farmers produced more than enough…for American consumers,"

Farmers markets are a great opportunity to buy fresh local produce and fresh baked goods. It's also a chance to speak with people who grow the food.

writes Robert F. Kennedy Jr. in his book *Crimes Against Nature*. "Study after study shows that these small operations are far more efficient than the giant farm factories. But agribusiness has used its political and financial clout to eliminate agricultural markets, seize federal subsidies, and flout environmental laws to gain competitive advantage." The average person may not have the power of a huge corporation but by working together, people can make a difference. If enough customers get together and ask for local food at their grocery store, the store may start carrying and labeling local produce. This can work at local restaurants, too.

TAKING RESPONSIBILITY

Parents feel responsible for choosing good food for their children's growing bodies. As young people grow up, they become responsible for making their own decisions about what to eat. It's hard to make good choices, though, when there are so many unhealthy options.

Around the country and the world, more and more governments are passing laws to help people make healthier choices. California passed laws in 2008 prohibiting public schools from selling soft drinks or high-calorie, high-fat foods during school hours. In 2007, New York City banned the use of trans fats in restaurants. Other cities, such as Boston and Chicago, are considering similar laws. In 2010, Santa Clara County in California proposed a local law to prevent restaurants from including toys with children's meals that don't meet US government nutritional rules for limits on salt, fat, and sugar. Ken Yeager of Santa Clara County says the law "helps parents make the choices they want for their children without toys and other freebies luring them towards foods that fail to meet basic nutritional standards."

Every dollar spent on food supports the food business. "The average American family spends almost half of all its food dollars on restaurant food, and each American consumer eats out at least five times a week," wrote Klein and DeWaal in *Dirty Dining*. It's up to everyone to decide if he or she wants to eat real food from farmers or fake food from factories. Local restaurant and store owners make real food available when their customers insist on real food choices, not just fake foods. Even corporations make changes to their factory food—better ingredients, better processing, less packaging—when consumers insist on eating real food.

10 GREAT QUESTIONS
TO ASK A NUTRITIONIST

1. How do I know if I have a food allergy?

2. What foods should I avoid?

3. How many times a day should I eat?

4. How many fruits and vegetables should I be eating every day?

5. Where should I look to find nutritional information when I'm eating out?

6. What are some good resources for healthy recipes?

7. How do I go about planning out my meals?

8. How many calories should I be eating each day? Where should I get those calories?

9. Should I never drink soda or fruit juice? Or is drinking them once in a while ok?

10. How can I limit my sodium intake?

GLOSSARY

allergens Substances (usually proteins) that cause an allergic response by the immune system, such as hives, swelling, stomachaches, hyperactivity, rashes, or problems breathing.

bipolar disorder A condition that is characterized by alternating depressed and manic states.

calories The energy your body gets from food. Carbohydrates and proteins have four calories per gram; fat has nine calories per gram.

carnauba wax A wax obtained from the leaves of the carnauba palm and commonly used in car wax, shoe polish, wood finishing, and low-priced candy bars.

chronic Always present, as in a long-lasting disease or condition.

diacetyl A chemical used in artificial butter flavoring, snacks, and bakery products. Tests conducted at the National Institute for Occupational Safety and Health (an agency of the Centers for Disease Control and Prevention) using diacetyl showed lung damage in laboratory rats.

E. coli A bacterium, *Escherichia coli*, that lives in human and animal intestines. Usually an *E. coli* infection causes mild diarrhea or no symptoms.

fiber Bulky cells in plant matter that can absorb water or give a tough texture to food. It is indigestible but necessary for digestion of other food.

halal Foods that are permitted under Islamic law.

hydrolyze To break down into components, as in hydrolyzed protein that has been broken down into amino acids. Hydrolyzed protein is often used to improve the flavor of foods and contains monosodium glutamate, a food additive.

kosher Foods that are sanctioned by Jewish law.

100-Mile Diet A diet that involves only eating food grown within 100 miles (161 kilometers) of one's home; this diet is promoted in a book by James MacKinnon and Alisa Smith.

pasteurize To use a heat treatment invented by Louis Pasteur in 1864 to kill germs in milk or other foods without influencing the flavor or quality of the food.

pellagra A disease that occurs when someone does not get enough niacin (a B complex vitamin) in his or her diet; victims can suffer skin sores, diarrhea, and mental confusion.

phthalates Chemicals, used to soften plastic, which have hormonelike effects on human and animal bodies.

salmonella A bacterium transferred from animals to humans through food that is not cooked thoroughly. It causes vomiting and severe diarrhea.

Slow Food movement Slow Food is an international nonprofit ecological and gastronomic organization promoting local food traditions; founded by Carlo Petrini in 1989.

trans fats Oils that have been hydrogenated (have had hydrogen gas bubbled through them) to make oil hard at room temperature by adding hydrogen atoms to the long molecule of fat. Trans fats have been linked to high blood sugar, high amounts of bad cholesterol and low amounts of good cholesterol in the blood, and also to obesity and cardiovascular disease.

vitamins Nutrients essential to the human body for health. They are found in fruits, vegetables, grains, fungi, meats, and dairy foods.

Action for Healthy Kids
600 West Van Buren Street, Suite #720
Chicago, IL 60607
(800) 416-5136
Website: http://www.actionforhealthykids.org
Facebook: @act4healthykids
Twitter: @Act4HlthyKids
Action for Healthy Kids works throughout the country to educate
people on the importance of healthy eating and exercise.
Their goal is to reduce childhood obesity.

American Diabetes Association
2451 Crystal Drive, Suite 900
Arlington, VA 22202
1-800-DIABETES (800-342-2383)
Website: http://www.diabetes.org
Facebook: @AmericanDiabetesAssociation
Twitter/Instagram: @AmDiabetesAssn
The American Diabetes Association is an organization focused
on educating people on diabetes.

Center for Science in the Public Interest (CSPI)
1220 L Street NW, Suite 300
Washington, DC 20005
(202) 332-9110
Website: http://www.cspinet.org
Facebook: @cspinet
Twitter: @CSPI
Instagram: @cspi_nutritionaction
CSPI is a nonprofit health-advocacy organization supported by
subscribers to its Nutrition Action Healthletter, with no indus-
try or government funding. CSPI led efforts to pass the law

requiring nutrition labeling and has publicized the nutritional content of many popular restaurant foods.

National Eating Disorders Association (NEDA)
603 Stewart Street, Suite 803
Seattle, WA 98101
(800) 931-2237
Website: https://www.nationaleatingdisorders.org
    NEDA is the largest nonprofit organization that works to pre-vent eating disorders and to help people who are suffering from them.

United States Department of Agriculture (USDA)
Center for Nutrition Policy and Promotion
3101 Park Center Drive, 10th Floor
Alexandria, VA 22302
(888) 779-7264
Website: https://www.cnpp.usda.gov
Facebook/Twitter: @MyPlate
The USDA Center for Nutrition Policy and Promotion website lets visitors set up a personal eating plan and track activity and eating levels, with recommendations for serving sizes, daily requirements, and eating plans to keep young people healthy.

World Health Organization (WHO)
Regional Office for the Americas
525 Twenty-third Street, NW
Washington, DC 20037
(202) 974-3000
Website: http://www.paho.org/hq
Facebook/Twitter: @pahowho
Instagram: @opspaho
The World Health Organization (WHO) is part of the United

Nations that works on health issues around the world. They publish many reports and articles about healthy eating and health issues related to unhealthy eating.

WEBSITES

Because of the changing nature of internet links, Rosen Publishing has developed an online list of websites related to the subject of this book. This site is updated regularly. Please use this link to access the list:

http://www. rosenlinks.com/FFTT/Factory

FOR FURTHER READING

Cohen, Robert Z. *The Stomach and Intestines in Your Body.*
New York, NY : Britannica Educational Publishing, 2015.

Eschilman, Dwight. *Ingredients: A Visual Exploration of 75 Additives & 25 Food Products.* New York, NY: Regan Arts, 2015.

Marchive, Laurane. *The Green Teen Cookbook.* Twickenham, UK: Aurora Metro, 2012.

Marlowe, Maria. *The Real Food Grocery Guide: Navigate the Grocery Store, Ditch Artificial and Unsafe Ingredients, Bust Nutritional Myths, and Select the Healthiest Foods Possible.* Beverly MA: Fair Winds Press, 2017.

Nestle, Marion. *Why Calories Count: From Science to Politics.* Berkley, CA: University of California Press, 2012.

Pollan, Michael. *The Omnivore's Dilemma: The Secrets Behind What You Eat.* New York, NY: Dial, 2015.

Rissman, Rebecca. *Processed Foods.* Minneapolis, MN: Core Publishing, 2016.

Tara, Sylvia. *The Secret Life of Fat: The Science Behind the Body's Least Understood Organ and What It Means for You.* New York, NY: W. W. Norton & Company, 2016.

Warner, Melanie. *Pandora's Lunchbox: How Processed Food Took Over the American Meal.* New York, NY: Scribner, 2014.

BIBLIOGRAPHY

Brandeis University. "New Fat, Same Old Problem with an Added Twist? Replacement for Trans Fat Raises Blood Sugar in Humans." ScienceDaily, January 18, 2007. http://www.sciencedaily.com/releases/2007/01/070116131545.htm.

Brooks, Megan. "Plasticizer May Be Tied to Boys' Breast Enlargement." Reuters, December 14, 2009. http://www.reuters.com/article/idUSTRE5BD39920091214.

Caughlan, Goldie. "TSP in Cheerios." PCC Natural Markets, June 2002. http://www.pccnaturalmarkets.com/sc/0206/goldies.html.

Deville, Nancy. *Death by Supermarket: The Fattening, Dumbing Down, and Poisoning of America*. Fort Lee, NJ: Barricade Books, 2007.

Ettlinger, Steve. *Twinkie, Deconstructed: My Journey to Discover How the Ingredients Found in Processed Foods Are Grown, Mined (Yes, Mined), and Manipulated into What America Eats*. New York, NY: Hudson Street Press, 2007.

Guyol, Gracelyn. *Healing Depression & Bipolar Disorder Without Drugs: Inspiring Stories of Restoring Mental Health Through Natural Therapies*. New York, NY: Walker & Company, 2006.

Kennedy, Robert F., Jr. *Crimes Against Nature: How George W. Bush and His Corporate Pals Are Plundering the Country and Hijacking Our Democracy*. New York, NY: HarperCollins, 2004.

Klein, Sarah, and Caroline Smith DeWaal. *Dirty Dining*. Washington, DC: Center for Science in the Public Interest, 2008.

Leiff, Cabraser, Heimann, & Bernstein, LLP. "New York Woman Files Suit Charging Butter Flavoring Chemical Diacetyl Led to Serious Lung Injury." Butter Flavoring Lung Injury. Retrieved April 10, 2010. http://www.butterflavoringlunginjury.com.

Mansbridge, Bruce. *The Complete Idiot's Guide to Conquering Obsessive-Compulsive Behavior*. New York, NY: Alpha Books, 2009.

Marler, Bill. "About Reactive Arthritis." About.com. Retrieved April

10, 2010. http://www.about-reactive-arthritis.com.

Nestle, Marion. *Food Politics: How the Food Industry Influences Nutrition and Health.* Berkeley, CA: University of California Press, 2003.

Nestle, Marion. *What to Eat.* New York, NY: North Point Press, 2006.

O'Reilly, Terry, and Mike Tennant. *The Age of Persuasion: How Marketing Ate Our Culture.* Toronto, ON, Canada: Knopf, 2009.

Patel, Raj. "Down on the Clown." Posted April 9, 2010. Retrieved May 20, 2010. http://rajpatel.org.

Pawlick, Thomas F. *The End of Food: How the Food Industry Is Destroying Our Food Supply—And What You Can Do About It.* Vancouver, BC, Canada: Greystone Books, 2006.

Pfeiffer, Dale Allen. *Eating Fossil Fuels: Oil, Food and the Coming Crisis in Agriculture.* Gabriola Island, BC, Canada: New Society Publishers, 2006.

Pollan, Michael. *Food Rules: An Eater's Manual.* New York, NY: Penguin, 2009.

Pollan, Michael. *The Omnivore's Dilemma: A Natural History of Four Meals.* New York, NY: Penguin, 2006.

Smith, Rick, Bruce Lourie, and Sarah Dopp. *Slow Death By Rubber Duck: How the Toxic Chemistry of Everyday Life Affects Our Health.* Toronto, ON, Canada: Knopf, 2009.

Taylor, Paul. "Small Doses." *Globe and Mail*, April 30, 2010, p. L1.

United Nations Food and Agriculture Organization. "Carnauba Wax Data Sheet." Retrieved April 10, 2010. http://www.fao.org/ag/agn/jecfa-additives/specs/Monograph1/Additive-109.pdf.

INDEX

A

additives, 4, 12, 22, 33
advertisements, 22, 33
allergies, 14, 25–26, 37
antibiotics, 7, 14

B

breakfast, 11, 12, 17, 30–31

C

calories, 29
  empty, 11, 15
  high-calorie foods, 36
  recommended each day, 37
cancer, link with diet, 22, 23, 24,
  27–28
candy, 4, 10, 16, 30, 32
cereal, 4, 7, 12, 17, 30–31
chicken, 7, 12–14, 22, 34
chronic conditions, 24, 28–29
constipation, 15, 17, 24

D

diabetes, 24–25
diarrhea, 19–20, 24
digestion, 15, 16, 17, 24, 25
dinners, 34–35

E

eggs, 4, 14, 31

F

fake foods, 15, 16, 17–18, 25, 28, 30,
  31, 33, 34, 35, 36
farmers, 35, 36
fast-food restaurants, 4, 5, 7, 10, 12,
  13, 22, 24, 25, 27, 28, 30
  companies, 33
  french fries at, 8
  hamburgers at, 7–8, 34
  packaging at, 20
fat, 5, 17, 22, 24, 28, 36
  fake, 17–18
  foods billed as low in, 4
  in french fries, 8–9
  in meat, 7
fiber, 10, 15, 16
food-borne illnesses, 10, 18–19, 20, 24
food poisoning, 24
  E. coli-related, 19
food safety, 10–11, 25–26, 33
french fries, 5, 7, 8–9
fruits, 4, 10, 27, 28, 30, 31, 32–33, 37
  sugar in, 16

G

gallbladder, 17, 24

H

hamburger, 5–6, 7–8, 13, 34
health concerns, of processed food,
  4–5, 6, 10, 13, 14, 17, 21, 24–26, 29
healthy eating, 6, 7, 12, 15, 16, 18,
  22, 23, 27, 30–31, 34–35, 36, 37

hormones, 7, 8, 13–14, 20–21

ABOUT THE AUTHORS

Julia J. Quinlan is a Massachusetts-based author, journalist, and editor. She has written numerous children's books on topics ranging from honey badgers to plate tectonics.

For twenty years, Paula Johanson has worked as a writer, teacher, and editor. She operated an organic-method market garden for fifteen years, selling produce and wool at farmers markets. She has worked as a short-order cook and as a sushi chef. She is the author of several nonfiction titles on science and health topics, including *Jobs in Sustainable Agriculture*, *Processed Food*, and *Making Good Choices About Fair Trade*. An accredited teacher, she has written and edited curriculum educational materials for the Alberta Distance Learning Centre and eTraffic Solutions.

PHOTO CREDITS